Contemplative Activism

Jessica R. Dreistadt

Contemplative Activism

ISBN 978-1537245164

The Fruition Coalition
Lehigh Valley, PA
www.fruitioncoalition.com
www.jessicardreistadt.com

Table of Contents

Introduction

Social and political activism is a means of authentically connecting with and engaging our deepest sense of purpose through reflective action. Activism reveals our convictions as well as our enacted commitments to our selves, each other, our communities, our nations, our planet, and our deities.

Why, then, does social and political activism so often fail to feel like spiritual practice? Why does it feel like a violent struggle through which ideological casualties are inevitably and unquestionably the ultimate outcome?

This book articulates and postulates a new paradigm of activism that is based on trust, hope, harmony, love, and peace. Contemplative activism is responsive rather than reactive, creative rather than critical, and compassionate rather than confrontational.

I'll be the first to admit that contemplative activism sounds like a utopian dream. We have been conditioned to expect and accept contention as the norm. But that just isn't good enough for me anymore; I yearn to practice activism in a way that consistently embodies all of my values.

Just a few years ago, I would have scoffed at the suggestion of contemplative activism. As a radical-progressive, I critiqued and contested the validity of views that were not within my vision. I agitated and manipulated to provoke alignment or agreement with my ideas. I was 'fighting for peace,' and feeling a growing disconnect between the world of my dreams and the means by which I sought to realize it.

We all have a raging activist inside of us, or some other pebble in the sole of our critical conscience. Such pebbles can either be a distraction or a means of provoking deeper and more clarified awareness. I remain a raging activist, but one whose flame invites and ignites the beautifully brilliant, inextinguishable, and illuminating light of love.

I feel called to pursue transformation; my soul whispers revolution. By choosing to nonjudgmentally listen to this voice, I can clarify my intentions and vision while creating space for a chorus of unlimited possibility to emerge. Like the eye of a hurricane, we can remain centered, open, and calm, but also very powerful, when we are in the midst of community and political turbulence. We can and should be the loving force that gently draws others in to a peaceful state of graciousness.

This book is an invitation for you to join me on a journey through some of the uncharted byways of social change. While *Contemplative Activism* is based on my experience, intuition, values, and inspired aspirations, your ideas and experience are essential for exploring this blossoming wilderness. Please enter this space as you are and interpret what you discover according to your own political position and priorities.

Let us begin.

Activism as a Positive Sum Game

Social and political activism is typically played as if it were a zero sum game. We negotiate and compromise, resulting in winners and losers. One person or group's gain is automatically a loss for the opposition. Zero sum games are based on cynical realism while positive sum games represent optimistic idealism. While both worldviews are valid, we can strategically choose how to interpret our circumstances to achieve the best results.

In positive sum games, relationships are dialogic rather than dialectical, leading to an expanded and even unlimited capacity for growth and transformation. Each player has something to contribute and by engaging in the process of play, everyone ends the game with more both individually and collectively.

Consider the following mathematical formula:

$$A + B \rightarrow A + B + C$$

In this formula, A and B are the players in one particular game. The players can be individuals or groups such as citizens, political parties, businesses, elected officials, PACs, or any other entity or combination of entities. C represents the extensive new possibilities that emerge through a playful, collaborative, and compassionate relationship between A and B. When A and B come together in this way, they create something more than themselves that could not otherwise exist.

In order to do this, A and B both need to lovingly reach beyond their immediate field of vision. In the beginning, A and B might feel disconnected and isolated; they may feel as though their interests do not overlap in any way. This assumption is most likely correct, but it is not sufficient to provoke meaningful and sustainable change. To pursue transformation, A and B need to courageously leap into the unknown, mysterious area that divides them.

After both A and B have jumped into the mysterious unknown and have spent some time swimming across the sea of possibility through cycles of dialogue and reflection, they will have more fully explored their options than they would have on their own.

As a result of this process, both A and B extend their vision and depth of perception. Their comfort zone expands. They find or intentionally create space where they can align or integrate their visions. Two disparate entities become united, yet remain unique.

The core of both A and B may remain constant. They may retain their original position. Neither needs to sacrifice their values or their convictions. By working together, they realize something original and unique that neither entity would have recognized without a relationship with the other. Both continually become more expansive, leading to greater unity across multiple entities. As more entities join the game, the dimensions of change multiply.

One political game that most people play is paying taxes. In this game, individuals and businesses that pay taxes represent one player while the IRS, as a representative of the government (in the United States), represents another player. We typically think of paying taxes as a personal liability. We write a check out to the IRS, or our liability is continually reduced throughout the year via payroll deductions. We involuntarily give up our money and the IRS receives it. We lose, and they gain. We can alternatively conceive of paying our taxes as a positive sum game. Rather than thinking of our taxes as a personal liability, we can think of them as an investment in our country, an investment to which most citizens contribute. Our focus shifts from what we personally have to lose to what we all have to gain as a nation by working together. The power and potential of our collective investment far outweighs the small individual contributions that we each make.

Whether or not we agree with the way our tax revenues are spent is a whole other story. Advocating for public policy changes or budget allocations can also be played as a positive sum game. When we speak with elected officials who appear to disagree with our position, we can compassionately and patiently engage in dialogue to reveal previously unexplored possibilities. In doing so, we don't give up any part of ourselves; rather, we become more of who we could and ought to be. We both do.

But we know it typically doesn't really play out like that. We meet in a group with people who think like us and/or share common experiences and develop an agenda; more often, an agenda is delivered to us without our input. We write that agenda on our hearts and pump it through our veins. When we meet with decision makers, we tell them what we think they should do. We ask them to share their position not out of sincere curiosity to provoke thoughtful dialogue, but as an opportunity to either gain their approval or expose their ignorance. We report this back to the agenda drivers and we check them off the list. To play a positive sum game, we need to enter relationships with an open heart and mind. Agendas block the flow of true, authentic progress and reduce natural human processes to mechanistic programming.

Playing a good game also requires a balance of offensive and defensive strategies. As progressive activists, we too often put ourselves in a defensive position. A will not be motivated to dive into the unknown mysterious area without the alluring provocation of B and vice versa. Rather than invite loss, we need to be leaders who model listening, learning, and loving so that we can all flourish. The more we offer, the more we will all have to share. As our minds and hearts expand and we become more open, we can develop a deeper understanding of social and political complexities and together we can realize beautiful possibilities.

Time

When I was in college, one of my professors proposed that time could either be seen linearly or as a circle. Alternatively, I see time as an outward, multidimensional spiral. Each moment expands upon the wisdom of the past. Cycles repeat, yet are clearly distinguished from what has happened in the past and what has yet to come. From my perspective, there is a pattern, a rhythm, to all of life; yet, the exact future manifestation of everything is miraculously nebulous.

The focus of activism is typically on the past or the future. With righteous indignation, we carry our grievances from day to day, year to year, and generation to generation. Over time, such grievances become ingrained, normalized, and magnified. At the same time that we critique decisions that were made in the past, we propose changes that we think will lead to different and better outcomes in the future.

Basing our activism on what has happened in the past provides an opportunity to express our feelings. It serves as a context through which we can interpret our experiences. The past also offers us a sense of familiarity, continuity, predictability, security, reassurance, and grounding. These are all vital processes through which we can learn, heal, and flourish.

At the same time, being too attached to the past can lead to escalation of negative emotions, resentment, guilt, alienation, and increased factionalism. This prevents opportunities for exploration, dialogue, learning, and creating.

Developing a compelling vision for the future can be equally valuable. Such visions can serve as inspiration, uniting and galvanizing people as they work toward realizing a better tomorrow. Yet, we can be equally attached to our vision for the future. This can lead to obstinacy, worry, fear, and disappointment. When we predetermine our future at a point in time that will soon become the past, we limit other possibilities and opportunities that will likely emerge through active introspection and interaction.

In activism, little attention is given to the present moment. Yet, the present moment is all that is real. Our interpretations of the past and the future are based on judgment and speculation.

Time is simultaneously microscopic and infinite. Within each moment lies the limitless potential of all time. There is no beginning and no ending. Each moment dissolves into the next and everything is continually renewed. Every moment reflects unique, unlimited possibility.

Activism is a living meditation through which we can intentionally cultivate awareness from moment to moment. We can be fully present, letting go of our feelings about the past and our expectations for the future, so that we can fully appreciate the pure sanctity of the moment that is upon us. We can value, and learn from, our past without being its servant. Rather than being attached to our vision for future, we can experience the anticipatory joy of optimism that continually fills our hearts with a deep sense of peace. By doing so, we become uniquely poised to enter relationships fully present as true partners who are aware of each other's needs and desires while also being open to exploring and nourishing those needs and desires.

Patience is particularly useful in social and political activism as it is a never-ending process with often unknown timetables. It can take years, or even decades, to create meaningful change that endures transitions in political leadership and priorities. And by that time, the needs of people and communities will likely be very different. If we were all mentally and emotionally in the present moment at least most of the time, our needs and the processes in place to fulfill those needs would be synchronized. Until that day comes, we must have patience. And we must have hope that such a day will come!

It is nearly impossible to think about being patient when people, animals, and the environment are suffering unnecessarily. I am not in any way suggesting that we sit back and patiently wait for change to occur. We need to be actively engaged in thoughtfully provoking change on an ongoing basis. But we also need to realize that one, two, or three conversations, essays, or events will hardly ever be enough to make change. Our effort needs to endure despite setbacks, obstacles, and ignorance. We also need to be patient with each other, recognizing that our past experiences and future dreams may be substantially different from what others hold dear in their hearts. And throughout the entire process, we need to remain mindful of the present moment so that our thoughts, actions, and words reflect the infinite potential therein.

Space

While political division in our country is fairly obvious, there is simultaneously an invisible divide that strongly influences our values and beliefs: our perspective on physical space and the nature of reality. We live in a predominantly Newtonian-oriented society. According to this perspective, all of life is linear and measureable. There are clear causes and effects. Therefore, it is possible if not preferable to isolate and control those causes to influence the outcomes. In contrast, a quantum orientation places a greater significance on complexity, chaos, spontaneity, and interconnectedness. Personally, I feel that there is value to both ways of seeing the world; however, we need to be aware of how we and others perceive matters because this influences how we all engage in social and political processes.

We sometimes neatly package ideas and then present them for approval or disapproval rather than allowing space for the splendid chaos through which exploration and transformation might occur. We continually try to isolate and minimize or eliminate the root cause of our problems, rather than concentrating our energy in a way that allows beautiful possibilities to naturally unfold. Our choice to be reactive versus proactive, creative versus compromising, constricting versus expanding, containing versus curious, and controlling versus cooperative are all in part rooted in our beliefs about the material world.

Our lives are cluttered with ideas, and we are strongly attached to those that most deeply resonate with our values and beliefs. Ideas may emerge from our own minds and hearts, or we may have adopted them from others -- perhaps adapting them to better fit our unique experiences, perspectives, and dreams. Ideas are intertwined with our identity, and the mere thought of letting them go can feel like losing a very special part of ourselves.

By detaching from our ideas, we are not negating them; we are in fact demonstrating the purest love from our hearts. Detachment is a suspension of judgment, or unconditional love. We can gently and carefully observe our ideas as something greater and more powerful than our own minds. We can seek a more profound understanding of the idea and how it relates to other ideas. When we detach, we do not claim ownership of or cling to ideas. We also remain open to continuous engagement with multiple, interconnected ideas that continually evolve in our individual and collective minds.

Our relationship with ideas should be like a good marriage. Our ideas should stick around because they have seduced us and reflect our most loving self, not because we have become entrapped. When we contain and control our ideas, or when we allow them to contain and control us, we become abusers of universal wisdom and victims of social hegemony. Thus, our ideas should be freely and lovingly shared with others.

When we detach from our ideas, we do not become disconnected from them. All things are interconnected. By letting our ideas go and setting them free, we have expanded freedom of movement which allows our minds and hearts to be drawn into emerging creative possibilities.

We sometimes superimpose ideas about material scarcity on our potential intellectual, emotional, social, political, and spiritual expansivity. Ideas are not a limited resource; they are infinitely plentiful and they are multiplicative. When we let them go we should rejoice rather than mourn; by doing so, they will likely gain momentum and become more brilliant than they were when we first perceived and conceived of them.

Our mind is like a window through which we view the world. Through contemplation and mindfulness, we can cleanse and purify our thoughts, returning to our true, innate state of peace, so that we can more clearly see our lives. As we become clearer in our thinking, the grime on the window of our mind floats away.

It takes a lot of courage to see past the grime of our assumptions, expectations, and convictions. We need to trust ourselves, each other, and the natural process of life to authentically see, experience, and feel as we engage in social and political activism. Detaching and opening up is a risk that demonstrates leadership. When we surrender with love and a strong core, we can have a clear conscience; when we surrender out of fear or apathy, our window is further muddied.

As we detach and become more open, we create a splendid state of spaciousness in which all things, all ideas, are possible. As space becomes more open, the speed through which ideas can change and spread increases as barriers are removed. In this lovely and loving space, we can feel the mysterious, gentle whispers that might otherwise be silenced. We learn how to listen to, be truly understanding of, and be responsive to, each other's hearts and minds.

Creating space through detachment is not enough; freedom is also needed for transformation and progress. If freedom isn't present, open space becomes a vacuum in which everything and everyone gets sucked into a particular direction by force. Freedom allows our ideas to flow and grow without inhibition.

Freedom must be universal; one person or group's freedom cannot impinge or be contingent upon another's. If you are not free, than neither am I. Freedom is a mutual responsibility. As we become more willing to accept responsibility, the freedom in our lives expands. Freedom grows out of respect, trust, love, openness, and reverence for ourselves and each other.

We sometimes forsake true freedom for illusory or imaginary freedom. Spiritual freedom, intellectual freedom, emotional freedom – these are all real. The freedom to easily choose from 30 different types of inexpensive toothpaste is merely a red herring.

Real freedom means we all have the opportunity to be and become who we truly are. It means we can happily and easily zoom in and out as we examine ideas with fluidity. It means we act from a place of joy and peace rather than fear and scarcity. It means we are able to effortlessly flow at every moment. It means that we can easily leap into the exhilarating freedom of the unknown, where all things are possible. It means that we are willing to risk the safety of what we know so we can soar into the delicious mysteries of ambiguity. It means that we are liberated from our fears, prejudices, and selfishness. It means that we are living in balance through love.

Energy

Power, love, compassion, wisdom, hope, and sincerity are infinite resources. Unlike finite or renewable resources which are depleted as they are used, infinite resources multiply when they are shared and they should frequently be used toward good ends. Infinite and finite resources should not be unintentionally interchanged; we should not have limited hope or love because certain material resources are limited.

Power is an energy that propels activism. We often focus on socially constructed power, or that which is rooted in our relationships and institutions. As activists, we must draw upon our natural power, or that which derives from the truest wisdom of our soul. Socially constructed power in not only finite, it is self-defeating. When individuals or groups seek to gain power by oppressing others in any way, even in defense, the whole is weakened overall.

When we engage in activism, we should do so from a position of infinite natural power. Otherwise, we subjugate our personal and collective power to that of those whose institutional power we are questioning. This unintentionally reinforces systems of inequality and blocks the progress of real, sustainable change.

Currency is both an exchange and a flow. It is a means of measuring value and a powerful rhythmic force. Anger and hope each have unique, dynamic currencies. The rhythm of the currency we choose will be reflected in the exchange that follows. Exchanges can have zero sum, positive sum, or negative sum results depending on whether they are resistant, resonant, or repugnant.

Harmony is just as important as rhythm. If we choose the highest frequency, we will likely drown out many lovely sounds around us.

Perhaps our goal as activists and leaders should be to create the most resonant symphony of sounds by harmonizing our voice with the nuance of others around us.

Being pulled toward something good is more powerful than being pushed away from something undesirable. Chasing a dream is more fun than catching a dream. Life is ever evolving and gently unfolding. Revolutions are a natural part of the ebb and flow of life. Every breath we take, every thought, every word, every gesture is a potential revolution. The very act of being alive is itself a revolution. Revolution is the natural process of life that continually beautifies and sanctifies our world.

Everything is impermanent. We are in a constant state of flux and transformation. Change is a natural part of life; it is life itself. Ideas and information flow without constriction when we are open, light, and free. When we choose not to slide across the surface, we can feel temporarily stuck in the messiness of complexity, unearthing details as we dig deeper. Being still and allowing this process to unfold creates clarity and synchronicity.

Resisting change creates pain. Resistance interferes with the natural, beautiful disorder of the universe. We are continually renewing and transforming individually and collectively. To not change is to cease to be.

Change occurs at many levels. For example, it can be institutional and related to policy or procedures or cultural and related to relationships and language. Change is provoked when awareness is heightened or when imaginations are stirred. This emerges through conversations, reflection, and other everyday intra- and interactions. Change can be observed, but interpretations of change may vary from person to person and from moment to moment. All interpretations of change and existence are legitimate in the hearts of their holders.

We can intentionally and continually unleash ideas, assumptions, myths, and practices through inquiry and dialogue and then let go to see what naturally unfolds. Through this process, we can cooperatively live open-ended lives with no right answers, no dogma, and no power struggles -- just peaceful bliss.

Nonviolence doesn't mean letting people walk all over us; it means restoring and maintaining interpersonal and social harmony so that we all have equal rights, access, and opportunities. When we let go of our attachments and live a peaceful life, we transform from struggling to suffering to surrendering. When we surrender, can be content without being complacent. That deep sense of purpose and happiness can ground our best work. We must be a living example to others we seek to influence, with our energies aligned to our most powerful and loving intentions.

Integrity

Feelings of fragmentation pervade political life. Living in a society governed by a predominantly two-party system reinforces a false sense of dualism, difference, and disparity. Not only are we divided by party or special interest group, we may also feel divided internally as we seek to align ourselves with others who most closely reflect our values, beliefs, and desires. It may seem as though we need to change, suppress, or let go of a part of ourselves in order to join with others for a cause.

Politics is organized by polarities. An individual can either support or not support an initiative. An elected official can vote for or against legislation. We can join one group or join another that is working in direct opposition to it. Our choices are falsely limited for the sake of simplicity and efficiency.

The social and economic issues for which we advocate are not at all simple and merit much more than efficiency; they are complex, dynamic, and critically important. We cannot simply choose a side, stand our ground, and feel that our work is done.

Each of us is a unique iteration of a greater, unifying whole. This whole is not simply divided into black and white, but is reflected in infinite expressions of the full spectrum of light through each of our souls. That which is in me is also in you, and that which is in us is also in what we have accepted as our political opponent. We are connected through spirit, through matter, and through action and those domains are in continual communion. All people, ideas, and things are interconnected. Every thought, every breath, every cell in our bodies are infinitely, intricately, and intimately intertwined, deriving from and nourishing the space we share. What we think, feel, and do becomes a part of us, of all of us.

What we think of as being in opposition to us is a reflection of something in our own soul. Ideas, things, and people that seem to repel us are actually a part of us. They are not only a part of our soul and spirit, they are also a part of the common social space that we share.

We typically think of politics as suppressing one part of this larger self so that another part can flourish. Rather than dominating and oppressing, we can seek to harmonize and balance. By integrating complementary ideas in an intentional and authentic way that reflects the highest potential of the whole, we can realize true, sustainable transformation.

Doing so isn't easy given the social space that we have haphazardly constructed over millennia. It requires patience, a suspension of judgment, and courage. We need to bring our whole, authentic and vulnerable selves into every social and political interaction. We also need to treat others as whole human beings rather than as the fragments we easily recognize. We need to remain calm, centered, and compassionate in even the most contentious circumstances. It means risking the safety and comfort of our ingrained convictions and opening up to unknown but unlimited possibilities.

We will never all agree, nor should we. When we pursue unity and agreement, there will inevitably be people who are left out. When we pursue integrity and accept difference, there will be a safe place for everyone. We complement each other to create the totality of humanity.

When we are disconnected, we become desperate and disparate. When we are aligned, we can feel secure and seamless. When we are integrated, we are free and flowing. Integration means movement, action, and gentle, continual cosmic transformation.

Intentionality

In modern western society, we tend to predetermine expectations, attempt to carefully control conditions so that we realize our goals, and hold ourselves and others responsible for outcomes. This process reflects strong cultural values that can be found in many of our economic, political, and social systems.

These ideas about change reflect a helpful paradigm, but the crux of change actually lies within. We can also change the world by purposefully changing ourselves. What we do, why we do it, and how we do it can change the character of the cosmos. By acting in accordance with the most miraculous aspects of our imaginations, we and the world will naturally progress. We don't always need a plan when we have purpose and passion.

We typically think that we can and should control things outside of ourselves. We fail to recognize how this oppresses others and impedes social and political change. Living in this way diminishes the sense of wonder and possibility that could otherwise inspire transformation. Solutions that emerge from within all of our hearts and converge within the social sphere are more highly transformational than those that are imposed by one group or individual upon another.

By being intentional, we can clearly illuminate the deepest desires of our hearts so that we can realize beautiful transformation through loving means. We can consistently integrate those desires into every thought and action so that we are intentionally living every aspect of our life purpose rather than reacting to the circumstances that others have prescribed for us. We can also lovingly allow others the space they need to express their hearts and souls without judgment or suppression.

To be intentional, we need to be self-aware. Every moment is a new opportunity to become and to be our true, authentic selves. Thoughts and emotion cannot be separate from action; our internal and external worlds are connected. Action is an expression of our intention. That which we feel in our hearts can be translated into every action, interaction, and decision.

Too often, we reactively calibrate our inner state to match how we perceive our external circumstances. We should shift our sense of control inward to our thoughts, feelings, and actions.

When we decide to do something or not do something it incidentally becomes a collective decision about the fate of our community. When we choose to be careful and intentional about what we think, say, and do, we begin to create a world that mirrors the dreams in our hearts rather than absorbing the pain of the world and unintentionally replicating that which we wish to eradicate. We can choose to actively create the world we want at any and every moment.

Relationships

Our culture lacks political and civil intimacy. The way we engage in activism can compound feelings of detachment, hopelessness, and despair rather than promoting a stronger sense of purpose, passion, and unity.

Activism is a relational enterprise. As social and political activists, we most often enter relationships with those whom we hope to influence from a position of ideological opposition. Without such differences, the need for the relationship would not be immediately apparent. Without the motivation to provoke change, we would likely not pursue these relationships but would rather focus our attention on building alliances and coalitions with others whose views were more similar to ours.

To influence others to adopt our point of view and to take a specific action, we use many tactics including informing, persuading, manipulating, negotiating, and sometimes even threatening. These tactics work and many important social and political changes have resulted from their use. Nonetheless, our repertoire of relational tactics need not be limited to those that attempt to restrain the freedom of others to think and feel independently or however they choose.

We can enter these relationships with a commitment to empathic appreciation and compassionate love for all people regardless of ideological, political, or other differences. We can commit to having relationships that are authentic and continually enriching rather than superficial and short lived. Rather than resenting others who appear to have more social or political power, we can use our real power to recognize the gifts that others have to share and the lessons that we can learn from them. We can treat them like complete human beings instead of as a convenient means to our predetermined ends.

When we accept others for who they are it does not take away from who we are or the ways that we have come to identify ourselves; it makes us more of who we truly are in our hearts. Just as we might resist others imposing their beliefs and values on us, people whom we seek to influence through activism might similarly shut down when we choose tactics over meaningful engagement. Perhaps the best way we can influence others is by guiding, supporting, and nurturing them as they intentionally reconnect with the purest places in their hearts.

To do this, we need to open ourselves up with humility, trust, and vulnerability. We need to let go of our attachments to ideas and identity, and forgive others for their mistakes. Doing so is a huge risk; we may feel as though we are jeopardizing the sense of solidarity that we have with our co-activists or that we are compromising our values. When we choose to value others, even those who are making what we consider to be poor decisions with dire consequences, we become a living example of the more peaceful and equitable world that stirs our souls.

Communication

When we communicate, we simultaneously dismantle the past while actively constructing the future. We can think of every word we speak as the beginning of miraculous possibility rather than as a process that solidifies what we have already accepted as the truth. Our language, like our thoughts and actions, should reflect the world we are trying to create. It should be superfluously affirmative and constructive. The more we express what we truly desire, the more easily it will become the norm.

Our social change efforts have three interrelated targets: ideas, systems, and people. Because these areas are connected and overlapping, we can easily misdirect our efforts toward the area that is most immediately apparent while unintentionally neglecting the other two. We sometimes interrogate other people rather than the ideas and systems whose impact far exceeds that of any individual person or group of people. Ideas and systems are complex representations of generations of thought and action. While they are deeply rooted, they are continually open to reinterpretation and reconfiguration by the people who experience and interact with them.

When we communicate with others, we should keep in mind that, like us, they are subject to the values that have been embedded in, and disseminated, perpetuated, and expanded through, ideas and systems over time. Through active reinterpretation of these values, both individually and collaboratively, we can provoke social and political change.

Values are communicated through story. We tell stories to ourselves and each other about our life experiences, our families, our communities, our nation, and the world in which we live. Stories are powerful expressions of cognition and emotion; they not only transmit values, they also influence the way we and those around us think and feel. One experience can be interpreted through multiple stories, each with a unique impact on potentiality. Through intentional reflection and dialogue, we can retell our stories so that they are inclusive, inspirational, and transformational. We create our world at every moment through our stories, our language, and other intentional expressions of our passion.

Communication should be about communion, or joining in common purpose through responsive interaction. Generative dialogue should replace debilitating debate so that we can collaboratively work toward meaningful and sustainable social change. When we debate, there are winners and losers. When we dialogue, we all have the opportunity to learn, grow, and expand our compassionate understanding.

Not only do we need to lovingly share our passion with others, we need to compassionately and nonjudgmentally listen to what they have to share. We may not understand or agree with everything, but we can use these conversations as opportunities to learn about ourselves, and how we respond or react to our environment, as well as about others who seem mysterious or even offensive to us.

When we enter into conversations with others, particularly those who do not share our values or priorities, we can express our curiosity through questions to open up dialogue. Questions can provoke both open exploration and greater clarity. Intentionally using questions promotes communion and creative exploration. It is fine not to have all of the answers, but it is unacceptable to not explore all of the questions.

Creativity

Rather than compromise when pursuing social and political change, we can collaboratively co-create. In communion with others, we can explore and develop policies and make decisions that truly reflect the deepest and most meaningful shared values.

We are responsible for actively creating the kind of world in which we would like to live. Creativity is the unlimited surprising, fun, and exciting emergent possibilities that surround us at every moment. It derives from a sense of awe, wonder, openness, and mystery. Creativity requires the courage to let go of what we have accepted as the truth so that we can learn as well as the vulnerability to authentically express our passion while simultaneously listening and responding to others.

The real success of achieving political or social change is the infinite creative capacity it unlocks and provokes. While such changes may better position us for a just and free society, the process of making those decisions strengthens the flexibility of relationships so that even more brilliant possibilities continue to flow through dialogue.

Learning is an ongoing everyday experience. Learning and change can be scary because it inherently implies detachment from currently held beliefs and understandings. It can be a threat to our individual or group identity. Alternatively, I see learning as an opportunity to grow. While we may choose to shift our position as a result of something we have learned, learning can also result in having a more expansive view or increased flexibility to shift our perspective. We can do both while remaining still in the same spot, in the safety of our core values and purpose.

Unlearning is even more critical than learning. We can't expect social change to occur if we ourselves are closed and static. We can reject absolute truth while accepting absolute love. Everything we have ever taken for granted should be carefully questioned. Our knowledge, assumptions, and beliefs are continually in motion.

When we cyclically unlearn and learn, we are being creative. We are detaching from our highly individualized base of knowledge and opening up to universal wisdom. We are hopefully creating the social and political changes we desire.

Concluding Thoughts

This very brief book has been an attempt to begin reframing the ways we think about and approach progressive social and political change. I hope that this book begins to shift the prevailing paradigm of progressive activism from one of division, brokenness, and despair to one of holism, integration, and love. We can respond rather than react, create rather than resist, understand rather than reject, harmonize rather than struggle, and love rather than fight.

I have planted the seed; now it is up to all of us to nourish and cultivate these ideas through both contemplation and action so that they can germinate and blossom. I'll see you in the garden.

www.ingramcontent.com/pod-product-compliance
Lightning Source LLC
Chambersburg PA
CBHW030551290526
45786CB00004B/1968